The Princess in a Woman

How a Man can bring out the Best in a Woman

The Princess in a Woman

By

Gilbert Chigozie Oguh

Dedication

This book is dedicated to my late parents

Joseph U & Anna A Oguh for the struggles

they went through

to help the ten of us, their children, have a

foot hold in life.

Papa and Mama. Thank you.

Wife Comment:

The love between a man and his wife should only grow stronger after the wedding night as God ordained. Rely on each other and avoid secrets. Let everything be on the table because relationship that starts with lies may not stand the storms of marriage (When the enemy steps in and challenges lurk at the door).

Faithfulness is not optional in a marriage because Christ our Lord is faithful. This writer, my husband, loves God. He heard from God about this book and ran with it.

This is what I know for sure about my husband, I can always reach him with the word of God. That is the one thing he never fails to respond to.

He is a great husband and a wonderful father to our children. He does his best, by the power of the Holy Spirit, to live up to the wonderful revelation God gave him in this book. I am happy and even happier on how this book is going to transfer relationships in families. After reading this book, your husband and wife relationship should be greater now than before.

Praise the Lord.

Anne N. Oguh

The daughter that Jesus loves.

Acknowledgement

I give all the glory to the Almighty God in The Name of Jesus Christ Who through the Holy Ghost inspired the Concept of this book into my spirit.

My thanks also to my precious wife who stood by me as this book was being written, encouraging and correcting me as I wrote. Honey you are the best.

Much thanks to the one person who literally forced me into putting this idea into a book form. When I shared with her what God has put into my heart, she went and bought one

USB for me, set the computer up for me and said, (START WRITING!). She also took it on herself to edit the entire book. Dr. IJ Agunanne, thanks a million. You will always be dear to my heart for making me do this.

My thanks also go to The Rt. Rev'd Dr. Felix Orji, OSB

Bishop of the Anglican Diocese of the West (USA & Canada).

Church of Nigeria (Anglican Community)/ACNA

Bishop, you took time to read the entire manuscript and put your honor on the line by endorsing the book even before I made the corrections you suggested. That shows great trust. Thanks.

Thank you so much Dr. Enoch Agunanne M.D. (Cardiologist)

From your summary of this book one would think you read it completely before I finished writing it. That goes to show your spiritual understanding of your fellow man as you understand their physical hearts and work on them. You are a well-balanced Christian medical doctor. God will always be your strength.

Thank you for the endorsement.

Thanks to you, Mrs. Karina Morales Cpht.

My co-worker and friend who did the

computer work for me.

I appreciate you.

Thanks also to the members of my prayer

group who welcomed the idea of the book

with much enthusiasm. God bless you all.

The Princess in a Woman

All Bible quotations, except where noted, are taken from **King James Version.**

Printed in the United States of America.

Foreword

Ann Kristin Carrol once wrote that, “If your wife looks like warmed-over death, has severe nervous problems, seems to have lost that youthful spring in her walk, the glow from her face, and somewhere along the way most of her respect, in 99% of cases you have a love ---starved female”.

Mr. Oguh in this book tells us that we can awaken the best in and recover the glow and youthful spring in our wives or fiancés or daughters by loving them and speaking words of affirmation and affection to them with persistence and joy. This book has integrity and trustworthiness because from my personal knowledge of the writer he actually practices what he has written in this book and has not been disappointed. I recommend the book to you"

The Rev'd Dr. Felix Orji. OSB.

Bishop of the Anglican Diocese of the West (USA & Canada).

Church of Nigeria (Anglican communion)/ACNA

Contents

Chapter 1

Depending on a Man

What does a MAN do to bring out the good qualities in a woman to make her be his helper? Let us hear God's Word on this.

In Ephesians 5: 23 -28 we read;

For the husband is the head of the wife, even as Christ is the head of the church: and He is the Savior of the body. Therefore, as the church is subject unto Christ, so let the wives be to their own husbands in everything. Husband love your wives, even as Christ also loved the church, and gave Himself for it; That He might sanctify and cleanse it with the washing of water by the word, that He might present it to HIMSELF (emphasis mine) a glorious church, not having wrinkle, or any such thing; but that it should be holy and without blemish. So ought men to love their wives as their own bodies. He that loveth his wife loveth himself. (KJV)

I believe that many of us may not understand what the Lord is saying to us in the scripture passage noted above. It is profound! Paul states that the Lord sanctifies and cleanses the church to present it to HIMSELF glorious and beautiful. So whatever the MAN is doing or going to do to bring out the best in his wife he is doing it for himself just as what the Lord does for His church He is doing it for Himself. In addition, the apostle states under the inspiration of the Holy Spirit that the man is the head of the wife. His role as head of the wife, like the Lord in relation to the church, involves leading the wife by nourishing, cherishing, and sanctifying his wife so she is glorious. That is what it means to exercise rule in the biblical sense of it.

But before we talk about it in detail let us see in the same Bible where God first ordained it that a created thing should rule and lead by bringing out the qualities in another created thing. That a MAN will sanctify his wife by his word.

In Genesis 1:16, we read “And God made two great lights; the greater light to RULE the day, and the lesser light to RULE the night; he made the stars also. Now what does this ruling by the lights mean?

Let us take the Sun for instance ruling the day. How does the sun RULE the day?

The sun pours out its light and heat upon the earth and by so doing it BRINGS out the beauty and potentials in living things. Flowers blossom, seeds germinate and energy is provided to the earth. The ability to blossom is in the flowers and the ability to grow and produce roots, stems, branches and fruits are in the seed but these abilities will remain inactive without the light and heat from the sun.

Is there any country in the world that had been or is being RULED by a Mr. 'SUN' politically? No. So the way the sun rules the day is by providing what is needed for the earth to function properly. Now have this in mind, the sun is the only one given this authority by God, nothing else. 'So only the sun can RULE the day.' This statement is the reason for this book. The sun does not rule the earth as we understand ruling but provides what is needed for the earth to function properly.

So when God said that the MAN will lead and sanctify his wife the woman it simply means that there are qualities in a woman which only a "MAN" can cause to come forth. It is the very kind of rule the sun has over the earth. Flowers blossom, seeds germinate and trees grow and bear fruits because of the sun shining on them. The sun didn't put these qualities into them but causes them to come forth by 'RULING' over them.

In the same way the wonderful potentials of the Proverbs 31:10-28, wife will only come forth when a 'MAN' speaks (shines as the sun) over her. Don't worry this will be explained or made clear as you continue to read.

In the plant kingdom, the seed has all the potentials of producing roots, stem, branches, leaves, flowers and fruits inside it but they will have to remain there and never come out unless the seed is planted. Once the water and sunlight come upon it, these potentials will begin to manifest otherwise, THEY WILL NEVER MANIFEST.

In other living things they need another kind of a stimulant. A Hen can lay eggs under the right light source but the egg will never produce a chick unless it was fertilized by a rooster. So the rooster rules over the unfertilized egg in that hen for it to bring forth a chick. It does not control the hen. One thing we MUST bear in mind is that it is determined that A ROOSTER will have to fertilize the egg but no particular rooster is mentioned. The potentials in a woman are like the eggs in her womb. They have to be fertilized by A SPERM from a human being in order to bring forth a human being. If the eggs are not fertilized by A SPERM, they will die and disintegrate. The eggs don't care whose sperm does the fertilizing. It could be a husband, lover, artificial or by rape as soon as it is fertilized, it is over. This is important as regards to the bringing forth of the potentials in a woman.

What this means is that A MAN has to bring out the qualities or make these qualities come out of a woman. The law in the plant kingdom is that the seed will have to be planted, it didn't say in a particular garden. Again the light will shine on it for it to blossom. It may be the light from the sun or an artificial light, all it needs is light. The plant will gravitate towards THE LIGHT.

So if that woman happens to be your wife, make sure you are the one giving her what she needs to bring out those buried qualities in her by being the one telling her she is beautiful, intelligent, hardworking, that she takes good care of the children (if you have any), that she is a good adviser, a wonderful friend, etc. But you may say, she is not all that, yes neither did you see the fruits in the seed until you planted it and the plant came out nice and good. If you don't do that and someone else starts doing it, she may, NATURALLY, like the plant gravitate towards someone's light. Then you will begin to complain that your wife is being unfaithful. Her character might be unfaithful, but like the plant looking for the light, she is just, naturally, going towards the stimulant for her hidden qualities. She does not hate you nor does she reject you it is just a natural response. She needs to blossom and "HER MAN" is not helping her. Always bear in mind that an egg has to be fertilized (if a chick is needed) and the hen can't do that by itself.

Again, it didn't say a particular rooster has to fertilize the egg. All the Hen requires to produce a live chick is a fertilized egg. This is the same in the pregnancy of a woman. Pregnancy can result from her husband, as was said earlier, it could be also from a lover, hobo, rapist, or artificial insemination, as long as the egg is fertilized, she will get pregnant. PERIOD. So why don't you be the one to bring the good qualities from your wife?

In many places where spouses still keep servants, gardeners, drivers, swimming pool cleaners, sometimes they find out, to their dismay that their wives are "taking to" (drawing closer) to these helpers. Why? Because these house helpers are the ones who sometimes tell her how beautiful, wonderful and intelligent she is and how beautiful the dress she wore the other day made her look. These may not be frequent comments but comments that are made to her from time to time. However the husband never noticed or simply ignored to tell her these. So, just like the seed seeking the sunlight, she naturally may respond to the stimulants. Wanting to hear more of those words.

Gravitating towards those men does not mean that she is going to jump into bed with them because they are activating the good qualities in her, far from that, most women have character, and they respect themselves, so, that is not what I am talking about here; that may happen but THAT IS NOT always the case. Gravitation may take the form of your woman giving more value to the words of that MAN than yours. It may take the form of her coming alive or brightening up more when that particular person is around and that may create suspicion in the mind of her MAN. She is not lewd, she is just responding to a stimulant.

The MAN may be saying I have put a good roof over her head, I have bought her a nice car, and she wears expensive jewelry that I bought for her. Well said but don't forget that if she is a career woman she can get all these by herself and for herself. She just wants you to be the MAN in her life.

Some women may accuse their men of not being romantic and the "MAN" will be thinking what she meant by that after they have had some kids together. As a matter of fact, for this is true, a fellow told a friend some years ago when him and his wife went to help them out in the challenges they were having in their marriage that one of the problems they were having was that his wife always said he was not romantic. He asked how he couldn't be romantic when they already had three kids then. So, this friend whispered to him when they were leaving to buy her some lollipops. This fellow actually went and bought some lollipops for his wife to prove that he was romantic! The problem here is ignorance of what to do and that is what this book is all about. I believe he would have done a better job if he would have started speaking those right words to her. Those right words will always keep the union together.

You may say, well that is flattery wait a minute; I was explaining this to a family friend, a well-educated young lady, a medical doctor, and I said, women should not consider this as flattery and she said," even if it is a flattery, that is what a woman wants to hear anyway." It is in a woman's nature that these qualities can never come out unless a

MAN calls them forth from her. It is the sun light she needs to blossom.

To some that does not make much sense. He might be thinking, how can she become more loving or helpful if I say she is even though she is not exhibiting that? God who made her that way also told us in the bible to call those things that are not as if they are and they will become. Didn't He also say the weak should say he or she is strong?

Our sciences or psychologies may not agree with that but we are not dealing with them, here, we are talking spiritual principles which are established laws. The spiritual principles operate by faith not by sight.

So let us stick with this spiritual principle that says that a MAN will speak the good qualities in a woman into action.

Do you want to know how to get this done?

See chapter two.

Chapter 2

Miracle or Process

Those who don't believe call things they can't understand miracles or luck. But those who understand the workings of nature know that the Creator made it to work in order and to follow processes. Our aim in life should be to understand how these things work, use them and then give thanks to the maker of all things. If the laws of gravity and lift were not discovered we would have no air travels today. Whatever things we are using or enjoying today are because the laws or processes about those things have been discovered.

One thing we must bear in mind is that when the law of lift was discovered, planes did not start flying the next day. Most of us have heard about Eddison doing so many experiments before discovering the light bulb. If he comes back to life today he will be amazed at the improvements and the different kinds of light bulbs that we have now. That is not just unique to the light bulb but it can be said the same of all inventions. Look at the shapes and models of cars we are driving today compared to what Mr. Henry Ford started with. Look at the radio, television, bicycles etc. to just name a few. What I would like to bring out here is that these things didn't spring out and filled the whole world the next day. They all followed processes.

This means that you must bear in mind that bringing out these qualities in your wife will also follow a process. Consistency, persistency and patience must be your guide. There is a joke about a man who texted his wife from work saying, "Honey you are wonderful, beautiful and intelligent and I love you." The woman got the text and said ok I will just wait till he gets back from work to tell me who the women is that he meant to send this message to. She thought that he mistakenly sent it to her. Why was she in shock? Because her husband had never said that to her again since their wedding. So when you start, be careful, pick your words and select the right time or times to say those words until she becomes used to them. Know that if you expose the little plant seeking the light suddenly outside on a very sunny hot day it will probably die. So be careful and know you are following a process. When the process is completed, people will start referring to the miracle in your wife's life or that you are lucky not knowing that it is not a miracle and luck has nothing to do with it. You made it happen by wisdom, understanding and help from Almighty God. When one gets this truth, of knowing the law behind an idea, and finds out the principle of operating it, that person discovers that there is no such thing as being lucky. The truth is that most of the time we follow principles ignorantly and they work because the law does not discriminate if you understand it or not. Climb a high building and jump off from there and see what happens whether you understand the law of gravity or not and age does not matter. This idea is new to you and to her so don't be discouraged just know it is the truth and that it works. And don't stop digging, you are just two feet away from your gold. Always bear in mind that it is a process and not luck that will establish this in her life. Miracles happen too from God. Just be patient.

Take your example from the lives of the scientists mentioned earlier, they continued despite failed experiments, times gone, money spent, (yes it cost them money), and probably from discouraging words from spouses who didn't understand them nor the vision they had in their souls. Your vision is to have the wife of Proverbs 31 and you will if you do not give up. You can achieve anything you put your heart to but you have to try, try and try again and you will make it.

To me a miracle is when God bypasses someone's efforts, that is, He cuts short the time it takes to come through but you have to apply the principle.

The principle may be laying hands on the sick, anointing with oil, praying etc.

You don't just sit down and wait, you need to do something. First you have to be determined to do it. Then give yourself a reasonable time frame and expect bumps on the way and go for it.

As we have been saying it is a process. Women are like juicy fruits with good seeds in them. The MAN can take the fruit, eat the juicy part and throws away the seed. This is seen in the depreciation of appreciation of the woman few months or in some instances years after the honey moon. The MAN forgets or is ignorant of the fact that the juicy part he ate was cultivated by someone probably the woman's father or uncle....MAN.... who kept calling her princess and wonderful till you got her. They developed those qualities in your wife for you. The man forgets that the seed left after he had eaten the juicy part of the fruit, when planted, will also produce many more fruits for eating and planting. Everything required to produce that juicy part again is in the seed he threw away or just ignored. If something is ignored, it normally goes bad or dies.

Give her the nutrients needed to produce those desirable qualities again by your words of encouragements, appreciations and praises and you will have more coming from her.

You can choose to go the other way too. Throw away the seed and nature will either dry it up or make it rot and hence kills it. Another thing that may happen to that seed is that some...MAN...may pick it up, nurtures it and begins to eat the juicy fruits again. That is what happens in divorce. The man must always remember that the cultivating of those qualities is a process and not a matter of being lucky. I emphasize this statement so that you don't quit so soon. Just know that if another man begins to cultivate those qualities after the juicy part is gone, she will naturally gravitate towards him. So divorcing her or ignoring her presence in the home is not the solution. If you....THE MAN.... do what you are supposed to do, you will have the peace and love reign in the home. Divorcing her, as is said, is not the solution here because her Maker says that it is dealing treacherously with her. Let us hear this directly from the Lord. The book of Malachi 2: 13-16 says; "And this have ye done again, covering the altar of the Lord with tears, with weeping and with crying out, insomuch that He regardeth not the offering any more, Wherefore? Because the Lord hath been witness between thee and the wife of thy youth, against whom thou hast dealt treacherously: yet is she thy companion, and the wife of thy covenant

15 And did not He make one? Yet had He the residue of the spirit. And wherefore one? That He might seek a Godly seed. Therefore take heed to your spirit and let none deal treacherously against the wife of his youth.

16 For the Lord, the God of Israel, saith that He hates putting away:(divorce) for one covereth violence with his garment, saith he Lord of hosts: therefore, take heed to your spirit, that ye deal not treacherously." KJV.

You see, He made you one so that you will bring forth a Godly seed or Godly seeds. So you enjoying the good qualities she came with, juicy part, and throwing away the seed, divorcing her after, is just like one who goes into a furniture shop, sees and enjoys the assembled furniture in the store and pays for it. The furniture arrives in his house in parts to be assembled and he did not do that. You saw how good it looked in the store (honey moon period) but you did not put the parts together in your house; will he blame the store for the malfunctioning of the item or for not functioning at all? Just “assemble” it and the beauty you saw in the store room will come out again. You need to assemble your wife!

Cultivating those qualities mean continuity of joy otherwise the joy stops. If you are preparing for marriage these ideas will help you develop a good marriage life but if you have been married for some time, it is not late and never late. As long as a seed is alive, it can be planted at the right season the difference here is that your wife has no season you can begin planting anytime.

Seeing the high rate of divorce in the world today makes it very clear that something is wrong. Why is it that people who loved each other so much as to get married, vowed that they would stick to each other until death do them part should part before the death? The reason is because the fire burned out. The juicy part was eaten and the seed was never replanted and nurtured. I am very convinced that if the simple principles revealed in this book are applied, there will be less break ups in marriages among couples.

So go to work, nurture the qualities in her and the beauty, the wisdom, the love will appear again. You can make your honey moon last as long as you want. It all depends on you……..THE MAN.

Chapter 3

Nagging

Most men complain that their wives are always nagging them. REALLY?
Did you try to find out why or did you just nag back? Some times that attitude may be due to social or hormonal changes in her body.
Let us take a look at this issue. A lady got married and she and her husband very much wanted a child of their own. For eight years, in spite of their efforts, nothing happened.
They literally gave up after those eight years.
Then

her wife started nagging and feeling depressed. The man felt it was because of the child issue and tried to encourage and even suggested that they go for adoption but the woman didn't change her behavior. Friends suggested that his wife might be pregnant and that he should take her to a gynecologist but he ruled that out because of past disappointments. After a while he decided to go and see a gynecologist and to his amazement, his wife was already three months pregnant. Good a thing he didn't try to medicate her during that time. What he needed to understand is that women react differently to hormonal changes during pregnancy and hence learned to navigate his way accordingly.

But if that was not the case, then let us go back to the plant kingdom. A planted seed, shielded from sunlight or any light, struggles to get that light. It grows fast and long with no luster but as soon as it gets the light, the growth becomes normal, the greenness appears and it starts to look beautiful. She is not nagging you, so to say, she is only crying out for deliverance. She wants to be recognized and appreciated. Have you noticed the change in her when a visitor comes in unannounced and says to her, "madam you look beautiful in that dress are you both going out for dinner or what?" Did you notice the change in her mood? The praise on her beauty works wonders.

Try this on a lady, wife, girl friend or daughter. You just walked in and noticed that she is angry or looks sad. Then you say to her, is everything ok? She snaps at you and says sit down there is something I want to tell you. Then say, ok, honey, but before you tell me anything I want to first of all tell you that you just look beautiful and I am very blessed to have you in my life. Now tell me what you want to tell me. Be sincere but even if it seems like flattery, as my doctor lady told me, that's what she wants to hear anyway in order to blossom.

It is just that by a woman's nature, where ever she senses that LIGHT, she grows towards it. The bible says that her desire will be on her man (like the plants desire the sun). Is it any wonder then that she is nagging you? You have what she needs to blossom. Have you noticed a woman crying or gloomy and you a MAN, asks her what is wrong? She replies, "I don't know you should know". Now in your ignorant of her nature will say how on earth can I possibly know? The point here is that she expects you as her husband to know. Why? Because she is caged in her emotions and wants to get out. Are you still in doubt why she nags you? You are her prince in shining amour

She is expecting you to speak those words that will make her bring out her wonderful qualities which only a MAN can do because she can't do that herself. She is just crying out for release. If you don't do it and you are her husband, and someone else does it, she may, NATURALLY, like a plant seeking the light, gravitate towards that MAN and you will say that she is unfaithful but it was all your fault.

To be fair the MAN is not always at fault when nagged. Look at this,

"Then David returned to bless his household. And Michal the daughter of Saul came out to meet David, and said, how glorious was the king of Israel today, who uncovered himself today in the eyes of the handmaids of his servants, as one of the vain fellows shamelessly uncovereth himself!

And David said unto Michal, it was before the Lord, which chose me before thy father, and before all his house, to appoint me ruler over the people of the Lord, over Israel; therefore will I play before the Lord.

And I will yet be more vile than thus and will be base in my own sight: and of the maidservants which thou hast spoken of, of them shall I be had in honor. Therefore, Michal the daughter of Saul had no child unto the day of her death." 2 Samuel 6: 20-23 (KJV).

What is being said here is that David was not wrong, yet he was nagged. David did not nag her back but explained to her why he did what he did. The great warrior refused to fight. What an example! For the Grace we have now, the Lord is not that severe but He knows what He will do to let her know the right thing to say. All you have to do is;

Trust in the Lord with all thine; heart and lean not onto thine own understanding. In all thy ways acknowledge him, and He shall direct thy paths. Proverbs 3; 5-6 (KJV).

So, knowing how effective your words are over her, be very careful of what you say to her or to any woman as the case may be.

What pulls your office secretary towards you? Do you remember the comment you made to her five months ago when she came to work in that new dress? You said that dress made her look pretty and you forgot it. Well she didn't. Ten months later she brought in the completed assignment you gave her to do and you said, you are a very wonderful intelligent pretty young lady. She banks that as well. Now she wants to hear you say more of those words so she begins to do whatever it takes for you to notice so she will continue to dress that way so that you will keep saying those words that keep blooming, looking beautiful and cheerful daily and your wife is looking moody and depressed because you are not speaking those things to her, (you should have been telling her these sweet things). Very soon, like a plant not getting the light, she is no longer what you used to see. She still is, only that it is now going atrophy inside her and only a MAN can bring it out, renew and replenish.

The relationship with your secretary may have started unintentionally and the poor lady does not even know what is making her react the way she is doing. Those words make her sparkle. That dress makes you look pretty, well she will make sure you see her wear it again. You are such an intelligent young lady. You may not have said those words in a week or months or recently but those words fertilize the qualities in her and cause her to gravitate more towards you. That will be the effect on her because it is from a MAN. And like the plant craving for the light, she will begin to look for more and more of those words from you. It is just the way she is created to react. She needs those activators of her qualities from a MAN.

God said that a woman will be that way and you can't change it just know your part and play it. Be warned that she is like a seed that will grow in any garden so make sure that your wife is growing in your garden, in your arms and not another's by supplying her those words otherwise you have lost her or you will only be living with a roommate and not a wife. I am not saying you should not appreciate a lady just be aware of the effects the words of a MAN has on her nature. Simply, she is designed that way. And it is not just any word you speak it must be those words that will activate her qualities that is the right chemistry. Let us take this as an example, you begin to talk about sports, stock market, politics or weather to a lady, she really doesn't care. She will be saying, I sit at home with my husband and he never speaks to me. Now you know why she is saying that. You should mix political talk, stock market talk with some sweet words for her too.

A physical egg, as we said earlier in a woman's womb, when fertilized with a MAN'S sperm will produce a human being no matter where it came from and by what means. All the egg needs is to be fertilized, that is its nature.

I am not against flowers but bringing her flowers don't activate her qualities. Some will take those flowers from you and trash them. Will the flowers speak for you? The woman needs to hear your voice and the flowers are a poor substitute. Speak to her on her birthday or on any occasion saying, honey, I don't think God made anything more beautiful, more intelligent or more loving nor a friendlier person on this day than you. That will worth more to her than a thousand roses. It will bring more radiance from her than any flowers or gold. Flowers are poor substitutes for words that come out of the mouth of a MAN for a woman. Have you noticed how the words on cards for ladies are framed?

Have you ever wondered why daughters gravitate more to their dads?

Who calls that girl, my princes, my lovely angel, daddy's baby? The father is making her (knowingly or unknowingly) develop the juicy part for her man in her future. We shall speak more on that later

The lesson here is that if you want your wife to stop nagging, then start speaking the right things over her. Wouldn't it be worthwhile if you start doing it today?

Chapter 4

"Praise" a fertilizer

Years ago when I graduated from high school, (I think Adam and Eve were still in the garden then, laugh out loud), I heard someone say that one could talk to plants and that they would respond. I became curious and wanted to prove that to myself. So being then in a country where it was very easy to find plants growing, I went to get some. I found two small pawpaw plants sprouting near their parent plant. I uprooted them carefully with a spade, dug two holes in our compound and planted them about four feet apart. I put the same amount of manure in the holes before planting them. Then I started watering them on the same days with the same amount of water.

What I did next was speaking over them. I was praising one, telling it how beautiful it looked and how well it was doing and that it was going to bear good fruits. I told the other one that it looked very sick and weak and that it would soon die. I did that for about three weeks or so. I was amazed at what I saw. At the onset they were both doing very fine then gradually the change began. They started reacting to my words. The one I was cursing started looking weak while the other continues to blossom. Finally the cursed one died and the one I was praising grew very healthy and after some time, as I continued to praise it, produced very beautiful pawpaw fruits. Someone may come up with one reason or the other why what happened did happen but my advice to such a one is to prove it for him or herself.

What I am trying to bring out here is the importance of praising the woman. She may not be manifesting what you are saying as yet but she will begin to do so with time. Remember that my pawpaw plants didn't respond in the first day or even the first week. Praise her for being very organized. Praise her for being a good house keeper. Praise her for being a good money handler. Remember that what you are doing is fertilizing these natural qualities in her for manifestations and growth. You must remember that if you, THE MAN, don't say these things, she may be drawn to the 'MAN' who says those things to her due to her nature. Every living thing responds to praise it is just that in this book we are looking at the effects of praise on a woman.

Even our creator, God, wants us to praise Him. Have you ever wondered why? I believe that praising Him will make more of His goodness manifest in the life of the one doing the praising. So it is your choice.

We praise and thank God for what we are believing and expecting and they come to pass but as long as one keeps complaining about the issue, it will remain there. It is the same way with the woman. As long as you,

(THE MAN), keep complaining about all these about her, there will be no changes. You can see as many counselors as you want, but it will be a waste of time and money. Just give life to all these qualities in her and they will come forth and grow. You are, THE MAN, the very image and likeness of God Almighty, and He has put this tremendous ability in you for the woman, use it. I advice 'THE MAN" who will try to use this knowledge wrongly that he is playing with fire, so to say. The time of ignorance has passed. So go ahead and bring out that virtuous woman of Proverbs 31; 10- 27 which ends in the 28th verse by saying; "Her children arise up, and call her blessed; her husband also, AND HE PRAISETH HER." (KJV).

In the above verse, who praises her? You, her husband. You see that is your God given responsibility. Don't push that away from you. Get the courage and nerves to do it. It may look a bit funny if not silly when you begin for both of you but continue doing that and you will be amazed in a short time how easy it is and how rewarding it will become. She may turn back to see if you are addressing someone behind her don't worry just remember you are bypassing her natural mind into her inner self who will be reacting to those things you are saying and will cause her to act. She has no control over that either. The way she is acting and will continue to act will be exactly according to your words over her. That is the ruling principle in her life. If you want her to change, then change your attitude/words over her too.

Find time to read that part of the scripture and you will find the hidden qualities in your wife. They are all in her, they were deposited into her, she was born with them however you have to play your part of bringing them out.

Your words of praise and encouragement give energy to these potentials in her and I mean you her MAN that she is supposed to depend on for the energy. The air, as cool and beautiful as it may be, will not give the seed the ingredient it needs to grow properly. The heat from fire will kill it instead only the light and its warmth is what it needs. Her fellow girl friends will not help her in this. They talk of what matters to them when they get together and we call that gossip.

Learn to make your wife a good reservoir for you for good advice, bring her up so that your heart will safely trust in her and she will do you good and not evil all the days of her life. She will rise up while you are yet asleep and give food to the whole house. She will make you look good in the neighborhood by helping the poor. Her mouth will be full of wisdom and in her tongue will be the law of kindness. She will make your house a home. Just read and see what you can do to help her bring forth.

Remember that acknowledging her and praising her will bring sun shine in your house and make it a home.

The bible says that we are made clean by being washed with the word and the blood. So wash her with good words and don't stain her with bad ones. Words are very potent. Just remember that we were created by the Word of God and saved by the same Word now in a flesh, Jesus Christ. Go and practice these principles and you will be glad you did. The bible says that knowing them is not going to do you much good but that you will be happy if you do them.

Again, I must bring this to the attention of any woman who may be reading this book. Please do not say what your husband is doing is cosmetic. Meaning it is not real. He is working hard to get used to it and you should try to help him with positive response. Telling him that he has been reading that book and not applying what he is reading will not be of much help to you nor him. Encourage him, knowing that this is for the good of both of you. If the children are involved, they too will benefit from the peace you both provide at home.

Marriage is beautiful, wonderful and exciting but like every other thing, you have to work at it.

Chapter 5

Rain of Praise

What do I mean by RAIN OF PRAISE? As much as declaring verbally
these qualities in her, the declarations make those qualities germinate and grow, praising her is another element you can't afford to miss in the process.

I have heard men complain that their wives are more interested in their children than in them and do you wonder why? Who praises her for that wonderful meal she prepared instead of just saying thanks after eating?

The kid will say, mom, this meal is just wonderful you are the best cook in the world and a wonderful mom. Who do you think she will make the same meal for next time? Your guess is as good as mine.

Always find a reason to praise your wife. You can never over praise her. In reality she deserves the praises. Praise her for the good advice she gave you regarding certain things in your life, which of course you ignored, and regretted later that you did. Praise her for managing the house right.

You may say that she is not doing all that, you may be right but remember that any quality she is not manifesting properly is because you, (THE MAN), have not given the light for its growth in her. Let us pause here for a moment and ask some serious questions. Should a man's inability or unwillingness to praise and admire his wife justify her bad behavior? Should she depend on her man's praise only to be good? Or should she be motivated by her commitment to Christ also? What is the place of the Holy Spirit in her life? Now these are questions that only the woman can answer but she can't do that without the Holy Spirit. So you the man should continue to do what you supposed to do which is believing and trusting in the law of process or growth. Praise does work wonders in many things, as the example I pointed out in the pawpaw plants I had planted. Right now, we are focusing on the effects of praise on a woman. Praising a woman will have positive effects on her appearance, her hormones and character. How can I prove that? Do it for yourself. You may be saying that you are just saying it but don't really mean it that does not matter. The sun pours its light on the plant not knowing what the plant is going to do with it. The plant does not know what to do with the light either but The Great Creator has made it in such a way that the elements in that seed will produce the plant with the effect of the light. In the same way those qualities in your wife know how to use the praises to produce the princess you are looking for. She is your helper. If you didn't need one, God would never have given her to you. You are therefore responsible for making your garden grow and produce the fruits you need for living. If you don't change what you are doing now, you will remain where you are but if you want to get to where you really want to be, then you must change what you are doing now to your wife. The only way you can change or improve the atmosphere in your home is not by forcing her or advising her to change but to change what you are speaking over her. In order words, "YOU SHOULD CHANGE."

Remove the speckle in your eyes first!

Have you noticed how detailed most women are? Sometimes this gets on the nerves of an ignorant MAN. Being a business man, I can't tell you how much money this quality has saved our business financially and in most dealings. So why don't you praise her ability in being so detailed? If she is not there yet, then do what we have been saying in this book. Pour your light on it that it may germinate and grow. I don't know why God put the things MAN needs to succeed in a woman and she desperately wants to see you succeed. She wants to give you those things but not knowing how because you have not activated her. It is just like your new credit card, you can't use it unless you activate it. Have you ever heard the saying that behind every successful man there is a woman? You may call that a spiritual principle or law but it is true. If you don't activate these qualities you will have to work too hard to succeed because it will be like trying to fell a tree with a blunt saw or axe and that demands more energy.

Why would you want to do that? You should rather let her give you the right materials you need to do the job, in that case, saving time and energy.

Some CEOS don't think they need the help that Almighty God has put in their wives to run a company and that may be the reason for repercussion with ulcers and high blood pressures. But I believe that there are wise ones out there who tap into that great resource and reap the wonderful benefits. So give her the credit for that or rain the praises on her and she will produce more. Praising her is just like pruning a plant so that it will produce more fruits, the Good book says. "As the plant can't eat its fruits but produces them for the planter, in the same way these wonderful qualities are for you....HER MAN."

Every well-developed woman wants to see her man stand out in any crowd. Whether the man is in politics, business or ministry it makes no difference to her she just wants her man stand out and will do anything in her power to see that is done. These may be negative examples but they prove the point,

Lady Macbeth and Lady Jezebel they stood by their MAN right or wrong. If any man will help his woman develop her God given abilities, he will have no reasons to be worried or suspicious of her as the trust will be there. The man's status out there elevates her status as well. The insights or advice she is giving you may seem small but if you apply them they will help you achieve great things. If you are married and have not been tapping from this great reservoir please wake up this sleeping giant and begin to do so but if you are not married yet, you have great insight on how to make your marriage work for you. In the first place this is what you will be doing to get her marry you so don't stop it when she does. You used it to make her gravitate towards you now you need to develop it and use it to be a great success in life. Don't expect someone else to do it for you. It will be like this story; don't remember from where I read it or someone telling me the story. The story is of a man whose wife had been suffering from depression for a long time. He had seen many doctors and all of the antidepressants the woman was given never seemed to work. The man was advised by some good friends to go with his wife and see a psychiatrist. After a few minutes of the man talking to the psychiatrist, he noticed the psychiatrist had praised the woman for her hair do, the way her dress was well ironed and how smooth her face looked. The woman brightened up and smiled for the first time in a long time. The husband seeing such a quick change in his wife was shocked. The psychiatrist told him his wife was fine and that what should be done to help her is just what he had done at least three times a week. To which the man thanked him, paid the fee and promised to send his wife to him three times a week for that. Don't be like that man.

Some men may be saying where can I start and what will I be saying?

You don't have to try to find out what to say, just say what the bible says about her. I have just picked out ten of them for you and you can just be giving them to her once a day until that one sinks into her mind and you take the next one. Remember this is for as long as you both live so don't be in a hurry nor discouraged. These are what you have to be telling her according to the word of God.

1. Honey you are a virtuous woman
2. Your price is above rubies
3. I trust you
4. You are always good to me
5. You do everything willingly
6. You take good care of this family
7. You are a wise woman
8. You are very generous
9. You make me proud among my friends
10. You are a very kind person.

Don't say you are not saying the truth, you are for the whole purpose is to activate these hidden qualities that she has. So, do it and keep doing it.

What part does the woman play in all these?

Let us go back to Him from Whom all these started;

“And the Lord God said, it is not good
that the man should be alone;
I will make him an help meet for him”. Gen; 2:18 KJV

The woman is his helper and should help him to accomplish his divine duty. She shouldn’t adapt the let me see what he is going to accomplish in this attitude. She should try to respond positively to as much as she can. If the two work together they will have a wonderful marriage and a happy home. It may be hard even harder for her to take it especially if the relationship has not been very friendly. Just know that the problem you are having had been because the right principles were not followed and for those hoping to get married, follow these principles and you will very much eliminate those problems.

Chapter 6

Be Sensitive to her Need.

This is an area most men have to be very careful with. Women may not like this analogy but I believe it is true in some instances. Look at and treat her sensitivity like that of a little baby. What do I mean by that? Little babies, in a crib, cry and yell for different reasons at different times. A baby may be crying because he or she is wet, hungry, or not comfortable with the lying position. The baby will not be able to tell you the reason for crying so it is your responsibility to find out.

The problem may be from her place of work. It may be social, that is a misunderstanding with one of her friends. It may be because of the spoon you left in the sink unwashed. In any case you have to carefully play the undercover agent. She is not stupid it is just the way she is made to be. “Her desire is upon her husband?”, Always remember that.

So what do you the MAN do? You must start probing. Do it carefully and with love. For instance let’s say both of you returned from work and you notice that uncomfortable mood or attitude in her, instead of yelling or getting angry yourself because you are also from work, you can just say, honey, dear, or however she likes you to address her, do you want me to make dinner tonight or will you prefer we go out for dinner? Or how was work today? Just do a little careful investigating. And I mean careful. Another thing the man can do is try and pull the strength out of her. She may be just tired. The MAN can just say, Honey, I don't know how you ladies do it. We both just came back from work and you still have the strength to go and prepare dinner, you are just awesome. That recognition and praise may be all she needs at that time. One thing I have learned in my thirty seven years of marriage is that women are very easy to be pleased if you know how to do it right.

A woman's desire is to have a sure place to attach herself. In desperation she clutches at the nearest and convenient thing even though she would prefer to cling to her MAN. Instinctively she knows her parents will not be there someday as naturally she ought to outlive them God willing. Her neighbors will also have to move someday. Friends are mostly for the time being and even her children will one day leave to pursue their own lives and only her MAN will be there with her. So you see why she wants that man to keep encouraging her and bringing out the best that is in her for him.

It is very important for you, The Man, to realize that making this woman develop is a duty her Maker entrusted into your hands and expects you to carry out that duty because He believes in you. You are not doing her a favor but developing in her what you need to succeed. It is called living for

one another as she needs you to develop and you need her to succeed.
It's like your two hands each one washes the other.

One other thing I have come to realize is that most women just want to know their MAN'S worth for assurance reasons. They really don't want the money but want to make sure that the money or security is available when needed. If you hide it from her, she will react in one of two ways. If she assumes that you have a lot of money, she will tend to spend far more than is needed thinking that you want to be spending it somewhere else and so wants her share. But if on the other hand she assumes that you don't have the money, she will be afraid and may feel insecure. If she knows your worth, she will control herself knowing that emptying out the purse spells disaster for the family and she is afraid of that. And the MAN should not be afraid as long as he keeps shinning the light on her qualities. But if the man says I don't trust her in letting her know my worth, it simply shows that he has failed to develop that quality of trust in her. That might make her tend to gravitate towards the MAN who will develop that quality of trust in her and who she can depend on. So it is very important for the man to be sensitive to her fears or concerns or whatever he wishes to call it.

Some women seem to gain weight after having babies, what should the MAN do in that case, criticize her for it? Remember she was not like that before you married her but became like that after so you contributed to it! What the man should do is to assure her of his love whether she is able to lose the weight or not, knowing that it is a very sensitive area in her life. This is something that most women are unable to control, try as much as they want. The MAN must be sensitive to that. If he continues to love her, encourage her and appreciate her, she will continue to do her best to bring down the weight but if she fails, well life goes on. But if the MAN insists, he must remember that there is someone out there who is admiring her calling out those qualities in her and who is willing to help her achieve her goal, so if she moves towards him, blame yourself. If also the man is honest, he will find out, looking at their wedding picture, that he does not look as attractive as he used to either for both have moved to another dimension in life. You must understand that your approval or disapproval as her MAN means the whole world to her not minding what anyone else says. So being sensitive to that kind of need is very important for a good marriage.

What is being said here is that the Man is responsible for developing those qualities so he should not run away from the assignment that her maker has given him to do. You must always remember that the greatness of a man is seen in the life of a well-developed woman and the beauty of a woman is from a man who knows how to bring out her qualities. For beauty is not only on the skin but in character as well.

Some men think that by working very hard and helping others while they have provided enough food and clothing for their wives is all they need. They seem shocked when the woman reacts differently to their belief. This is common to some Men of God. They say, I am doing the work of God, preaching the gospel and saving souls and that does not seem to move her. Well, that is good for her spirit but don't forget she also has her emotions, (Soul and Body). If her spirit only is fed and the others ignored, there will be problems. Please be sensitive to that as well. Don't come back from ministering telling her of how many souls were won for the Kingdom only and neglecting her famished emotions. Don't think she is not happy with what you are doing it is just that she needs feeding as well. Look around the house and praise her for keeping it in order. Praise her for her patience while you were away. Just find something to praise her and if you can't find something to praise her, then open your eyes wider.

The woman's values in some cases are quite different from that of the man. Most women are just not interested in the man's sports or politics.

I heard of a survey, (not quite sure the survey source), conducted by a company after the assassination of president Kennedy. The women, I am made to understand, were asked what they thought would happen. Their concern was how the wife will handle the children alone. "Poor Jackie", they said. The men on the other hand were worried about who will handle the Cuban missile crisis. That was during the cold war. So as a man you must try to see things through her eyes sometimes. Be sensitive.

Chapter 7

Navigating Away

Another thing that will help you in the marriage, as a MAN, is knowing how to navigate away from potential problems. I don't know how scientific the saying is, but I am made to understand that women speak more words a day than men. When that talking time comes don't try to out talk her for you just can't. Tell her, "Honey, why don't we sit down and talk this over?" In that case you apply the idea of the board room method suggested in chapter nine of this book. Time will be saved, friendship and love maintained If you apply that method.

It is said that most marriages get into trouble because no real talking is done. People don't take the time to find out the facts but rather they take the neighbor's words or some other person's for the truth. Take this case for example, and this is an incident that really took place. This didn't take place in this country, USA, but in another country, which I don't intend to mention here. A man had worked with a company for several years but he and his wife couldn't afford a car. Because of his dedication to this company and loyalty, the company bought him a brand new car. This was a thing of joy to this family. One day he was driving back home from work and this lady asked him for a ride and he took her to her house. A neighbor saw the lady in the car and went and told his wife before he got home. When he got home he took his meal and went to bed to get some needed rest. While he was resting, his wife in her rage and anger, went outside and burnt the car. Neighbors asked her why she was doing that, she explained that the car has now become a problem as her husband is now using it to carry his girl friends around town, bragging. The man didn't say a word but the next day he called his wife's family for a meeting to discuss the issue. In the discussion, the wife found out that the woman her husband was giving the ride was her own (the wife's) sister who needed a ride home from a bus stop. That would not have taken place if she had talked to her husband instead of believing her neighbor. The man, here, navigated away from a bigger problem by holding his words. Sometimes the way money is spent is a big issue. For instance one may have the habit of over spending. In this case the solution is not fighting over it but talking about it and coming up with an agreeable answer. Don't ask your neighbor for the solution to your problems. The marriage is between you and your spouse and not between you, your neighbor and your spouse. I sometimes wonder why some spouses go to seek advice from some MARRIAGE COUNSELORS who are themselves divorced. Does that make any real sense? Both partners must learn to navigate away from looming problems.

Please I am not saying here that people should not see counselors what I mean is that people should, like in many other things, choose wise counselors.

There are several ways, a man can navigate through a challenge. Let us take a look at some of those ways with some examples. A man had a very happy marriage, living beautifully with his wife who has gone to be with the Lord. But there was one issue in the marriage that troubled the man which many people may call minor, but it was of concern to him and he dealt with it in a very wise way.

It was the way the toothpaste tube was used. The wife was used to squeezing the tube from the middle and the man did not like it. He brought it to her attention several times but the woman could not bring herself to change the habit.

What he did was buy two toothpaste tube. One for each. Miracle! Problem solved.

Another example involves a man and his wife as well, the wife did not like how the man treated their restroom commode.

She felt the man was not conscious of the fact that she too uses it. They had a big house she had a half bath for visitor.

So, the man decided to use the visitors' commode. Another miracle! Problem solved. So find out what you as a man can do to resolve those minor issues instead of fighting over it.

The MAN must remember that he does not have to answer every question nor comment on every statement the woman makes. Some questions have to wait for some time before being answered and some comments have to wait before being responded to. Some of the comments are just for the man to listen to and some of the questions are food for thought for the man.

If some negative comments are being made about some of your friends, it will be a very good advice to listen instead of defending them because women have this ability to sense things that men desperately need. Sometimes their messages are coded and you have to have a discerning spirit to catch what the message is. A popular musician once sang a song and in one of the lines he said that you should watch your friends when you are in love with or married to a beautiful woman. That negative comment made about those friends that seem irrelevant to anything you can think of may be coded warnings. Moreover, are they not husband and wife's talk?

So what is being said is that another way to navigate through a dangerous situation in your marriage is to pay good attention to the under tone of your wife's talk. When you both join some group of friends, observe your wife's attitude, mood and talks, she may be giving you very good signals if you have helped her develop herself. Always remember that she is with you to do you good and not evil. If you understand that and adhere to it, that may help you out of many problems. In otherwise, learn to trust your wife period. Forgive me if the emphasis on this is too much in this book, but I know it to be very true, most men are very easy to be pleased. I am told of a preacher who once told his wife, that he could not understand why God made her so beautiful but with little intelligence. To which the woman replied that God made her beautiful so that he the husband will love her and made her less intelligence, so she could love him. I guess in mathematics, that is a balance equation.

Chapter 8

Love Renews Youth

The bible tells the MAN to love his wife as Christ loves the church. What does that mean and how can THE MAN do that? How did Christ love the church? Christ said; "Greater love hath no man than this, that a man lay down his life for his friends". John.15;13 (KJV) How does His laying down His life show that He loves us? What did that do for us? By what He did, we are now sanctified, justified, made holy, and saved. You can find this in Hebrews chapter 10. If you look at verse 10 of that chapter it says," By the which will we are sanctified through the offering of the body of Jesus Christ once for all". This means He brought out holiness, sanctification, righteousness from us because these have been marred by the "sin nature" we got from the devil. If you are from those places where men hold the opinion that women should be seen and not heard or you have that concept yourself, I have two words of advice for you. WAKE UP! Remember we were created in God's image meaning that Godly attributes already exists in us and they needed to come out or we needed to be renewed. That is why a born again human person, in Christ, is called a new creation. So the love of Christ renewed us.

Let us go back to where this praising of a woman by a man started. Abram had lived with this old woman, Sarai, for many years and she could not bear him a child. God told him to start calling her Sarah, (PRINCESS MOTHER OF MANY). God was revealing to Abraham a principle, which if followed, will renew the youth of his wife and make her productive. God didn't go against His established law. He just revealed to

Abraham how to apply the principles that will make that law work, which is this, "Abraham, start speaking over her." Today we all know what happened when he did that. Remember that he had a choice. He could have said; "what is the use after all the woman is too old anyway. It is the same as you saying we have been married for so many years and she is so set in her ways, what is the use? Biologists tell us that there are seeds that have remained dormant for hundreds of years but as soon as they are planted, they germinated and grew. She is no different, just begin to speak over her. Plant her in the right garden of praise and you will be amazed.

That word, from a MAN, renewed Sarai's youth and in less than a year, she was able to bear a child in spite of her age. She was able to bear a child despite her age. She became fruitful to him because of what she did. So, will your wife be, if you begin to speak those constructive words over her. Christ said, I love you and when the spirit of any person receives that, the person is renewed. As long as that person will begin and continue to say, like John in the bible, I am the one that Jesus loves. So renew the youth of your wife by telling her that she looks young and beautiful. Renew her intelligence by telling her how wise and knowledgeable she is. Tell her she is strong and attractive and she will begin gradually to manifest these buried attributes. Remember we were not what we now are until Christ presented us faultless before the Father. Now we are all trying to live up to that. Your wife will become what you call her. The beauty you saw in her that made you marry her, was put in there by someone else who helped her develop that beauty; like the sun helps the plant to develop. Now that you are in her life, don't cut off that light or she will begin to wither. Is it any wonder she is no more attractive. So, like the sun, give her like the plant, the light she needs to grow. Speak into her life the good words. The majority of men do speak into the lives of their wives but they speak the wrong words. Words that cause them to wither and finally die. They die in creativity, beauty or glamour. A woman was created beautiful and that beauty will always remain in her so reactivate it with your words. Remember what Adam did when God presented Eve to her. Grandpa Adam lost his breath. “THIS IS THE BONE OF MY BONE AND FLESH OF MY FLESH”.

The MAN should renew the youth of his wife by speaking the right words over her that she will continue to look beautiful to the point that he will be willing to die with her. Your wife was beautiful, that was the main reason, I suppose, you married her if she is now ugly, it is your fault. Renew her youth and beauty.

Am I being hard on men? Well I am one of them and have been married to the same woman for thirty seven years at this time of writing so no one can say I should wait and see. I even have a grand kid so hold your peace about my being inexperienced. The truth is that experience has nothing to do with this. I have heard of people divorcing after thirty or forty years of marriage because they are ignorant of this truth. Don't be one of them. Renew your wife daily.

One of the problems that prevents men from doing this is pride. Trash that pride, humble yourself and enjoy a wonderful relationship with your wife. Divorcing her is not the solution because the next woman you are going to get involve with is not going to remain at that age forever. That woman will also need your help to get developed and if you have not learned to do so with the previous woman you had, how do you expect the new one to work with you. If kids are involved that is another disaster. You must take into consideration the pain it will cause those kids now and in future. No matter how much money you leave them, if you have that much, they will always miss the unity of their parents. You must take into consideration the pain it will cause those kids now and in future. No matter how much money you give them, they will always miss the unity of their parents. If you doubt that take a look at the statistics of young males in the prisons today. So for their sakes, learn to solve that problem and live happily. There are no doubts in our mind that any marriage can be beautiful, if one begins to put these things into practice. It is a matter of choice, a hard one for the men but a necessary one for the family

Chapter 9

Develop Her Potentials

Someone gets hired in a job when it is believed that the person in question has the needed training for that job. If the person does not have it, the person is either trained or asked to go and get the training. In many professions today we have the ones who have the needed training and we have the technicians. These Techs are the one who simply carry out orders from the trained ones. They are not held responsible for big mistakes by the higher authority. Not much intellectual input is needed from them. Don't make your wife a technician in the house. Develop her potentials so that she will be a real equal partner. If all she does in the house is carry out your orders, then she is simply a technician in the house and you are the one losing. Some technicians have the answers to the problems faced in some companies but they are sometimes not used because they are not recognized. For example there was a story some time ago of why we have some elevators now being outside the building instead of inside. I was told, as the story goes, that a building was going on and the engineers wanted a position to install the elevator and because of the nature of the building they couldn't come up with a suitable position for it. They had worked on this project for months and it was known among all that that was the problem they were facing. So one day the garbage man, or someone who had no building engineering degree, asked them why not put the elevator outside the building. That was the answer to their challenge and the reason we have some elevators outside some buildings today. It was good that they didn't ignore that suggestion. So develop the potentials in your wife she might one day help you put the elevator outside the building and you will notice that it works perfectly well. If you read the bible remember the story of the Syrian leper, Naaman. He was a great army general who was trained to give orders to privates and not take it from them. He was so big to himself that he refused to take the order of the prophet to go and deep seven times in the Jordan River in order to be cleansed of his leprosy. But when he listened to and took the advice of one of his servants (technician) and did what the prophet asked him to do, he was healed. How many men today are going around with financial leprosy because they have not developed their wives potentials. How many businesses have failed because the MAN refused or didn't know he had to develop his wife's' potentials.

So as the farmer will not let the seed remain in his barn but will take it and plant it in his garden because he expects to harvest its fruits, do so with your wife. Otherwise she will remain in your house (barn) and you will be hungry of the good things buried in her. Some men become abusive to their wives because they believe she is not contributing to the keeping of the house. Well whose fault is it? When she told you to be careful of some friends of yours did you listen? When she advised you against that failed investment did you listen? When she talked to you about that unmarried or married secretary of yours about her observations according to her female instincts did you listen? See the results of your ignorance or pride and now you are asking for forgiveness and taking your frustrations on her by being abusive. As was said earlier, if the MAN had all it took to make it in life, God wouldn't have given him a helper. Remember that the helper was given him before the fall of man not after. That goes to show that no matter how wise the man thinks he has become, he needs a helper.... THE WOMAN..... In that case you see the wisdom or ignorance when a man says, "I'm a self-made man." If that

man will take the time to calculate what it cost him to be that self-made man without the help from his WOMAN, he will not like to do that again. Could that be the reason most women outlive their husbands because men spend their days trying to be self-made when The Almighty God gave them a helper? So you see that developing those potentials in her will make her look, younger, healthier and more helpful to the man and add more days to his life. When God said that her desire will be on her man and that she will be a helper to him, we must understand that every word of God is a law or principle that is established forever. Therefore, in order not to eat by the sweat of your brow, develop her potentials and she will render the needed help to you. If not, she will always seem frustrated and you will continue to be aggressive. This is one of the reasons why the verbal or physical fights erupt. If the verbal fights seem to be around the corner, there is a way to handle that. During these fights, each wants to drive his or her points through. All one hears are loud voices and much talking which none understands. You spend hours on this and by the end no one knows what the other said nor can he or she recollect what was said. There is a way to handle that issue and you will find out that

you will solve the problem in thirty minutes or so for what would have taken you hours and frustrations to solve. My wife and I took our example from board room meetings. In a board room meeting everyone is given a time to express his or her opinion and no one is expected to interrupt. So when we expect one of those conversations that might be heated, we take a piece of paper and pen each and sit by a table with one of those clocks with large numbers on its face and moving minute and hour hands. We decide how long each will have to speak usually three to five minutes and when one is talking

the other is not going to interrupt. If one finds a reason to interrupt that one writes it on the piece of paper and waits for his or her turn.

When one's time is up, according to the clock, that one stops and waits for the next turn while the next person picks up from there. If you finish your points before your allocated time you can ask the other person to go ahead. In most cases the problem is solved in less than thirty minutes with a kiss. No raised voices nor grudges. Try it believe me it works I speak from a thirty seven years of marriage experience. So go ahead and develop her potentials. Create a happy marriage and enjoy it.

Chapter 10

Marriage Made In Heaven

From what we have read so far in this book the MAN may ask, if I have to do all these to bring out the princess in my wife what about the saying that marriage is made in heaven? That is very true but there is a catch to that and I am going to explain that to you.

Marriage made in heaven is like pieces of a puzzle in a box with the beautiful picture of whatever it will be when put together on that box. You get the box with the picture on it and the pieces in the box. So now it is your choice to continue to look at the picture on

the box (marriage made in heaven) or put the pieces together and have the real object with you, (marriage as it should be on earth but packaged). In this case apply the suggested principles and get a good marriage. Every piece you need to make that lady the helper she is made to be is in her and you will have to put them together.

Let us look at two examples of this puzzle being put together from the bible. God said to Moses; "And look that thou make them after their pattern, which was shown thee in the mount". Exodus 25: 40 (KJV)

This was when God showed him the tabernacle in heaven and asked him to make it on earth as he saw. Moses had the picture in his mind; "tabernacle as it is in heaven". It would not have done him nor anyone else any good if he had not instructed for it to be put together, that is constructed on earth. He would have been enjoying tabernacle as it is in heaven, picture, and never having it on earth.

Another example we have from the bible is the description of Jesus Christ as the Lamb slain before the foundation of the world. If Christ had remained in heaven as the Lamb slain before the foundation of the world, no one would have been saved. He had to come and put the puzzle of that picture together on earth for it to be realistic.

I don't want to weary you with what this puzzle,(the lady), will look like when put together but let me wet your appetite a bit with one or two things the bible says about her in Proverbs 31;10-31. The bible says that, in her, is a virtuous woman, meaning that she is of a noble character. It says she is far above rubies, that is, she is priceless, it says that her husband trusts in her this means that she will make you have confidence in yourself. She will do you good and not evil all the days of her life. I said I was only going to wet your appetite with

what you have in your house as a wife. Don't say that is not my wife. Well that is the picture on the puzzle box now put the pieces together to get the object. That is marriage made in heaven and you have that marriage. Some of the things we buy these days come in pieces in containers or boxes with the instructions on how to assemble them and the picture of what the things will look like if (PROPERLY) assembled. In some cases, the individual is unable to assemble the object. In that case you ask for help. So do the same thing in this instance. Ask God to give you all you need to bring out this beautiful person she is. Remember, you are not making her what she should be rather you are assembling her, meaning you are bringing out what she already is. That furniture, good as the different pieces are, can't assemble itself because it was not made to do so. It is the same thing with your wife, she was not designed to do it by herself. There is one thing I must bring to your attention in this case, she is a living person and not an inanimate furniture. This means her assembling must be continuous. You can't do it for six months or three years and say you have done enough then that living furniture will break down and will need some serious repairs. Whatever you have not been giving life in her will begin to shrivel and eventually die if you stop. Let me give you an example of how living things respond to stimulants for that is just the part you are playing in this case. I have some flower plants in my compound. One day, I saw that one of the plants looked as if it was about to die. The flowers and the leaves looked withered. At a closer look I found out that the sprinkler head giving it water had been moved away from it by the person who did a yard work for me. All it needed was water and that water supply restored. Now it does not get water on daily basis but on constant routine so that the soil will not get dry. When it got dry the plant, by its appearance, brought it to my attention.

A woman, by her nature, will bring it to your attention that you are slacking in your responsibility. She might start being moody or irritable if that happens, begin again to shine the light on those qualities that are meant to help you. Begin telling her again of how intelligent, helpful, beautiful and precious she is bearing in mind that by her nature she will always gravitate towards the stimulant and produce for the stimulator.

I believe enough has been said in this book to make you have a beautiful and fulfilling marriage. This is the way God made women to be and the part you have to play as THE MAN to bring her to her full potentials. Before the fall she was simply your helper but after the fall she had to depend on you to be that helper so you need each other.

The only thing that will stop you from doing this is if you can't speak or you are too proud to do so. This is a challenge to see if you have what it takes to bring forth a virtuous woman from your wife and have a wonderful marriage. If you are consistent in practicing what is suggested in this book, you will be amazed to what you will see in a very short time.

Enjoy a happy marriage.

Author's Commentary

Thanks for taking the time to read this book. I

believe you will find some help from it or

know

Someone you can help with what you have

read in this book.

This book can be used in many ways to help

others like in small

prayer groups or in marriage counseling in

churches.

You can also give this book as a gift to any

person getting married

or already married you will be helping them

in future challenges.

In a nutshell, you will be evangelizing. If you can help get this book into the hands of just two people after you have read it, you have done a great job in spreading the principles put forth in it.

One more thing before I let you go, please if you can write one or two positive statements regarding this book on Amazon it will encourage others
to take a look at it. Just log on to
http://tinyurl.com/reviewdiscipline
and write in your comments.

Thanks for helping save families.

Chigozie G. Oguh

For bulk copies please contact

Grace Pharmacy

11140 La Quinta Pl.

El Paso, Texas. 79936

Or call 195 593 0603

Endorsements

When I saw the burden in Minister Oguh's heart to write this book! I knew I must encourage him in any way possible to put it to print. From the very moment Minister Gilbert Oguh and his wife Minister Anne Oguh sat down with me and described what God laid in his heart while they were on a cruise, I was confident that once this book gets out, so many homes will be changed for good. Everything this Minister's wife(Minister

Anne Oguh) wrote on the wife's comment section about her husband is true!

When I read her comment, I remembered a story about a man who was being buried. And before they would put him into the ground, so many people said a lot of nice things about the dead man. At a point, the dead man's wife started opening the casket of her dead husband.

The Ministers who were officiating rushed the woman and asked her, "Ma'm, what do you think you are doing?" The dead man's wife said out loud that she was trying to make sure that whoever was in that casket was indeed her late husband as all the good things being spoken about him were NOT true!

Who else knows her husband well but her---the wife.

Because Minister Anne has testified that what her husband has written indeed comes from her husband's heart, then there is no hesitation but to endorse this book!

Please grab your copy and save a marriage or even yours today.

There is so much insight and knowledge that Minister Gilbert has brought forth through this book. I am certain that this book will bless even generations to come.

To Minister Gilbert, I say write more as the Lord leads you.

Pastor IJ Agunanne (MD, MPH, BCMAS, MBS,PH.D)

Founder 3Dimensional Women Conference-One SMART chick

Co- Founder of Jesus Club International.

Co-Pastor Royal Dimension

"The Princess in a Woman" is a very insightful and profound book that is full of useful guidelines for those who want to enjoy and not endure their relationships.

Minister Oguh takes readers on a thoughtful but truthful walk through the world of women and understanding of what it takes to bring out the best in them.

Just like many people seek expert advice to inform their major decisions in areas like finance and career, so should men endeavor to seek ways to nourish and cherish the women in their lives, in line with Ephesians 5:29.

This book is a key that unlocks many practical ways to release, celebrate and coronate “THE Princess in a Woman”.

-Dr. Enoch Agunanne, MD

Co- Founder, Jesus Club International

About the Author:

Minister Gilbert Oguh is a Registered Pharmacist in El Paso Texas where he works in his pharmacy, “Grace Pharmacy.” Gilbert is married to Minister Anne Oguh, his wife for 37 years! They both have 3 blessed grown up children; Chigozie, Ifeanyi, Ijeoma and a granddaughter named Noel

Gilbert and Anne are the Founders of Winning by Grace and Faith ministry.

Their Christian show (Good news from El Paso) airs regularly on KSCE TV El Paso Texas.

88198327R00095

Made in the USA
San Bernardino, CA
12 September 2018